# GRUMMAN
# F8F BEARCAT
## Christopher Chant

Foulis

Haynes

**A FOULIS** Aircraft Book

First published 1985

© **1985 Winchmore Publishing Services Limited**

**ISBN 0 85429 447 3**

*Published by:*
**Haynes Publishing Group**
Sparkford, Yeovil,
Somerset BA22 7JJ

**Haynes Publications Inc.**
861 Lawrence Drive, Newbury
Park, California 91320, USA

*Produced by:*
**Winchmore Publishing Services Limited,**
40 Triton Square,
London, NW1 3HG

Printed in England

Further titles in this series will be published at
regular intervals. For information on new titles
please contact your bookseller or write to the
publisher.

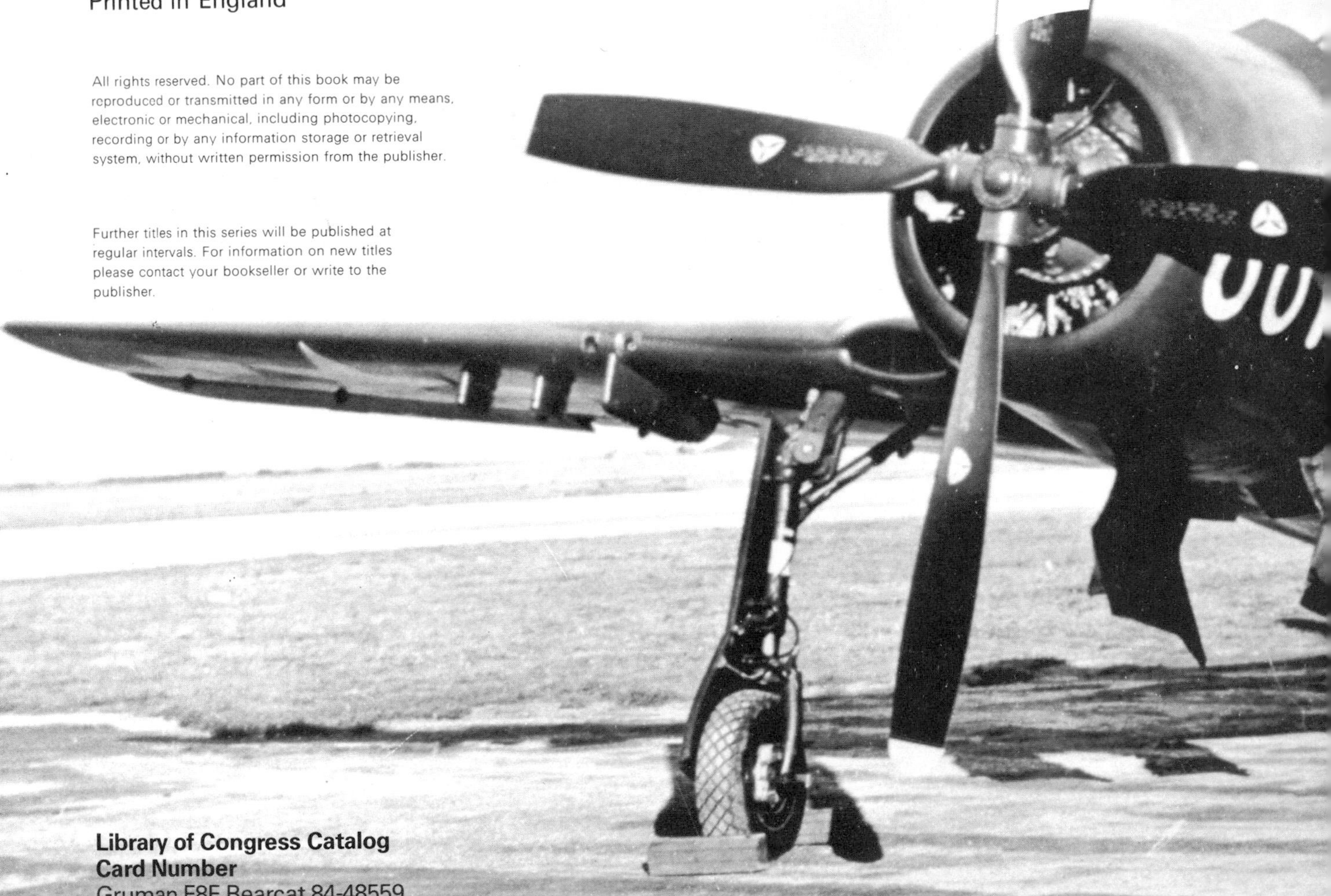

**Library of Congress Catalog
Card Number**
Gruman F8F Bearcat 84-48559

# Contents

# Genesis

The Grumman F8F Bearcat was the last piston-engined fighter accepted for service with the US Navy, and was undoubtedly one of the high points in the development of such aircraft despite the fact that it had been rendered obsolescent by the time it began to enter service in 1945. Thus the Bearcat enjoyed a first-line service career of only five years with the US Navy, providing its aircraft-carriers and attendant task forces with magnificent low- and medium-altitude air cover in the period that marked the rapid development and widespread deployment of the first turbojet-powered combat aircraft.

The genesis of the Bearcat can be traced to the time of the United States of America's entry into World War II, when the US Navy's standard fighters were the Brewster F2A Buffalo (being phased out of service as it was a first-generation shipboard monoplane fighter and thus only of indifferent performance) and the Grumman F4F Wildcat. The latter was an altogether more capable machine produced by Grumman and then, as the FM in a number of variants, by General Motors (Eastern Aircraft Division). The Wildcat (a name applied only later in the type's service) was typical of the 'Grumman Iron Works', whose products had already served in what were for the time large numbers with the US Navy: it had a portly fuselage matched to the diameter of the large radial engine, with the retractable landing gear designed to retract inwards and upwards into the

*Left:* Grumman's first monoplane fighter for the US Navy was the F4F.

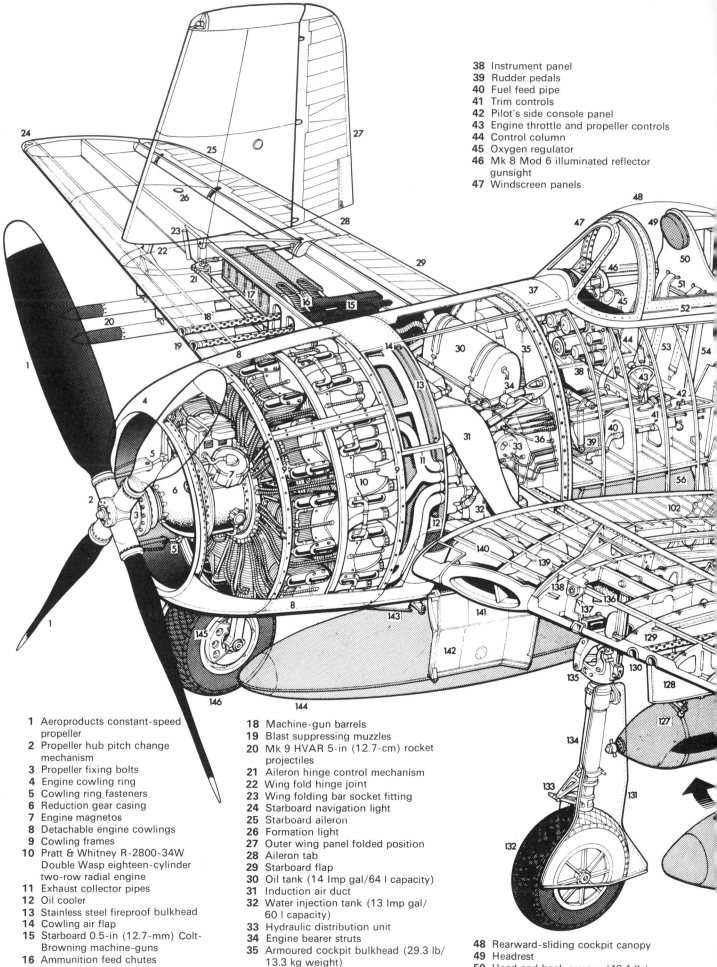

38 Instrument panel
39 Rudder pedals
40 Fuel feed pipe
41 Trim controls
42 Pilot's side console panel
43 Engine throttle and propeller controls
44 Control column
45 Oxygen regulator
46 Mk 8 Mod 6 illuminated reflector gunsight
47 Windscreen panels

1 Aeroproducts constant-speed propeller
2 Propeller hub pitch change mechanism
3 Propeller fixing bolts
4 Engine cowling ring
5 Cowling ring fasteners
6 Reduction gear casing
7 Engine magnetos
8 Detachable engine cowlings
9 Cowling frames
10 Pratt & Whitney R-2800-34W Double Wasp eighteen-cylinder two-row radial engine
11 Exhaust collector pipes
12 Oil cooler
13 Stainless steel fireproof bulkhead
14 Cowling air flap
15 Starboard 0.5-in (12.7-mm) Colt-Browning machine-guns
16 Ammunition feed chutes
17 Ammunition tanks (300 rounds per gun)

18 Machine-gun barrels
19 Blast suppressing muzzles
20 Mk 9 HVAR 5-in (12.7-cm) rocket projectiles
21 Aileron hinge control mechanism
22 Wing fold hinge joint
23 Wing folding bar socket fitting
24 Starboard navigation light
25 Starboard aileron
26 Formation light
27 Outer wing panel folded position
28 Aileron tab
29 Starboard flap
30 Oil tank (14 Imp gal/64 l capacity)
31 Induction air duct
32 Water injection tank (13 Imp gal/60 l capacity)
33 Hydraulic distribution unit
34 Engine bearer struts
35 Armoured cockpit bulkhead (29.3 lb/13.3 kg weight)
36 Engine control runs
37 Access plate

48 Rearward-sliding cockpit canopy
49 Headrest
50 Head and back armour (49.4 lb/22.4 kg weight) see 54

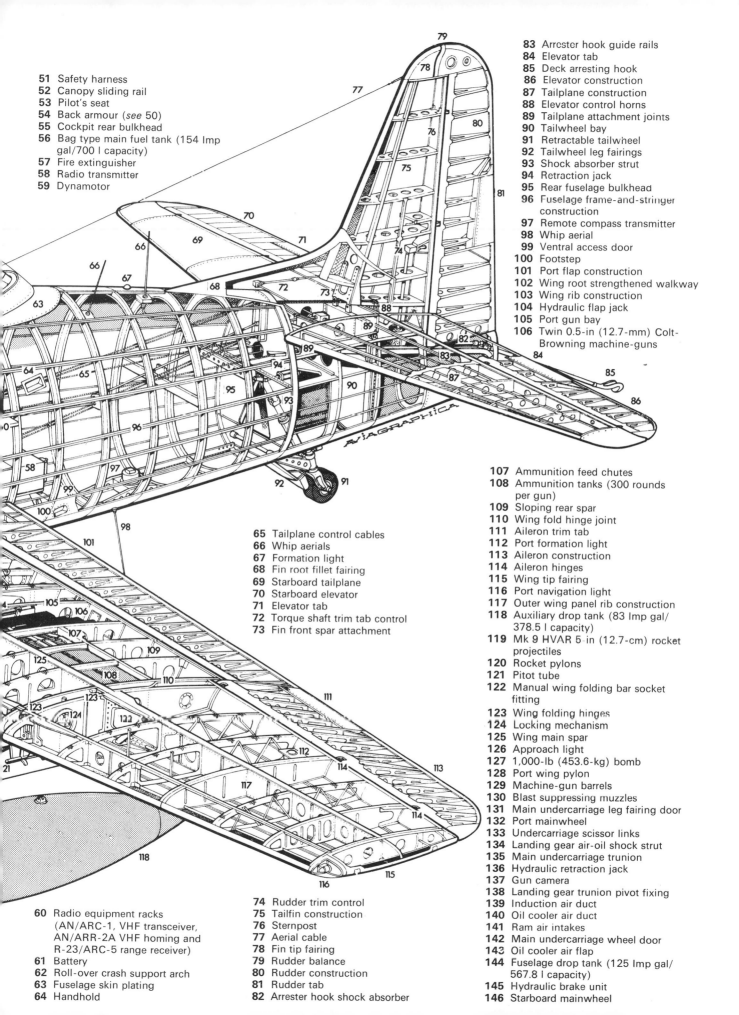

51 Safety harness
52 Canopy sliding rail
53 Pilot's seat
54 Back armour (see 50)
55 Cockpit rear bulkhead
56 Bag type main fuel tank (154 Imp gal/700 l capacity)
57 Fire extinguisher
58 Radio transmitter
59 Dynamotor

83 Arrester hook guide rails
84 Elevator tab
85 Deck arresting hook
86 Elevator construction
87 Tailplane construction
88 Elevator control horns
89 Tailplane attachment joints
90 Tailwheel bay
91 Retractable tailwheel
92 Tailwheel leg fairings
93 Shock absorber strut
94 Retraction jack
95 Rear fuselage bulkhead
96 Fuselage frame-and-stringer construction
97 Remote compass transmitter
98 Whip aerial
99 Ventral access door
100 Footstep
101 Port flap construction
102 Wing root strengthened walkway
103 Wing rib construction
104 Hydraulic flap jack
105 Port gun bay
106 Twin 0.5-in (12.7-mm) Colt-Browning machine-guns

65 Tailplane control cables
66 Whip aerials
67 Formation light
68 Fin root fillet fairing
69 Starboard tailplane
70 Starboard elevator
71 Elevator tab
72 Torque shaft trim tab control
73 Fin front spar attachment

107 Ammunition feed chutes
108 Ammunition tanks (300 rounds per gun)
109 Sloping rear spar
110 Wing fold hinge joint
111 Aileron trim tab
112 Port formation light
113 Aileron construction
114 Aileron hinges
115 Wing tip fairing
116 Port navigation light
117 Outer wing panel rib construction
118 Auxiliary drop tank (83 Imp gal/ 378.5 l capacity)
119 Mk 9 HVAR 5-in (12.7-cm) rocket projectiles
120 Rocket pylons
121 Pitot tube
122 Manual wing folding bar socket fitting
123 Wing folding hinges
124 Locking mechanism
125 Wing main spar
126 Approach light
127 1,000-lb (453.6-kg) bomb
128 Port wing pylon
129 Machine-gun barrels
130 Blast suppressing muzzles
131 Main undercarriage leg fairing door
132 Port mainwheel
133 Undercarriage scissor links
134 Landing gear air-oil shock strut
135 Main undercarriage trunion
136 Hydraulic retraction jack
137 Gun camera
138 Landing gear trunion pivot fixing
139 Induction air duct
140 Oil cooler air duct
141 Ram air intakes
142 Main undercarriage wheel door
143 Oil cooler air flap
144 Fuselage drop tank (125 Imp gal/ 567.8 l capacity)
145 Hydraulic brake unit
146 Starboard mainwheel

60 Radio equipment racks (AN/ARC-1, VHF transceiver, AN/ARR-2A VHF homing and R-23/ARC-5 range receiver)
61 Battery
62 Roll-over crash support arch
63 Fuselage skin plating
64 Handhold

74 Rudder trim control
75 Tailfin construction
76 Sternpost
77 Aerial cable
78 Fin tip fairing
79 Rudder balance
80 Rudder construction
81 Rudder tab
82 Arrester hook shock absorber

underside of this massive fuselage; it was immensely strong; it was adequately armed with four (later six) 0.5-in (12.7-mm) heavy machine-guns; and it was characterized by a mid-set wing structure.

Though well pleased with the F4F, the US Navy was much surprised at the beginning of World War II by the overall superiority of the Imperial Japanese Navy's standard shipboard fighter, the Mitsubishi A6M Reisen (Zero). In terms of overall combat performance the A6M was not in any way markedly superior to the F4F, but it was armed with two 20-mm cannon and was a magnificent dogfighting platform. American naval pilots went confidently into the fray with their F4Fs, but were shot out of the skies as they attempted to dogfight with the nimble Japanese fighter, whose presence came as a rude shock to the Americans despite the flood of warnings that had been sent

from China during the late 1930s and early 1940s by Claire Chennault, the US leader of the American Volunteer Group serving with the Chinese force of Generalissimo Chiang Kai-shek. The Japanese had with utmost sense blooded their new combat aircraft in China in the long-drawn effort to conquer that vast country, and at the same time had built up a small but highly competent cadre of experienced naval pilots able to wring every last drop of performance out of their excellent aircraft. Though the chances for air combat over China were small, the pilots of the Imperial Japanese Navy had evolved highly advanced combat tactics admirably suited to the unique nature of their fighters, which combined much of the biplane fighter's agility with the performance advantages of the monoplane.

Their initial losses served to teach the US naval aviators how to deal with the A6M while

flying the F4F: the primary conclusion reached by the US Navy pilots was never to dog-fight with an A6M, which was a far more manoeuvrable aircraft, but rather to make slashing attacks from a superior height and then climb in a zoom, the F4F's dive and zoom climb characteristics being superior to those of the lighter A6M. Later in the war the relative merits of the two types were quantified after comparative trials had been flown in the USA between an FM-2 and a captured A6M5, and these conclusions were invaluable to fledgling fighter pilots. The main points of the comparisons were the generally superior speed of the A6M5 at heights above 5,000 ft (1525 m), the see-saw superiority of climb rate between the two types (with

*Right:* Successor to the F4F was the F6F using the same design concept but adopting extra size and power for additional performance.
*Below:* Advantages of the F4F type were compact size and adequate performance.

the A6M5 superior in the vital band between 4,000 ft/1220 m and 13,000 ft/3960 m), the similarity of dive and zoom climb rates, the superiority of the A6M5 in the turn (where the A6M5 was reckoned to gain one turn in eight at an altitude of 10,000 ft/ 3050 m), the comparability in roll rates (with the A6M5 superior at speeds below 178 mph/286 km/h), and the generally greater manoeuvrability of the A6M5 at speeds below 205 mph (330 km/h). The conclusion offered to the US Navy pilot flying the FM-2 was to tread warily, avoid a turning encounter, maintain a height advantage and if attacked from behind roll and dive into a high-speed turn.

With such tactics the pilots of increasingly potent F4F/FM variants were able to obtain a parity with the ubiquitous A6M series by the end of 1942. But to wrest overall superiority from the A6M and its successors (and the US Navy sensibly anticipated the arrival of such successors which, in the way of things, should be considerably more potent machines) required a successor to the F4F. This was already on

the drawing boards, as the F6F Hellcat, at the time of Pearl Harbor and was recast to incorporate the lessons dictated by early combat experience with the F4F. The Hellcat was from the same basic mould as the Wildcat, but slightly larger, considerably heavier and far more powerful, and in the event turned the tide firmly against Japanese fighters with its combination of strength, fire-power and performance. Interestingly, the same tactical conclusions about combat with the A6M5 were reached with the F6F-5 Hellcat, the definitive production variant, it being considered inadvisable ever to enter a turning combat with the A6M5, or to follow an A6M5 into a loop or roll; the F6F-5 pilot was advised to use the superior speed and dive/zoom climb characteristics of his air-craft to gain the combat edge on the A6M5. Thus the tactics open to the F4F and F6F pilot were almost identical, the pilot of the F6F having an advantage over the pilot of the F4F in the generally superior performance and protection of his aircraft. The F6F-5 was also a more flexible

aircraft in operational terms, the model being built specifically as a fighter-bomber able to carry two 1,000-lb (454-kg) bombs or six 5-in (127-mm) rockets in addition to its inbuilt armament of six 0.5-in (12.7-mm) machine-guns, which were devastating against the light and relatively unprotected structures of Japanese fighters, in which light weight was deemed essential for the promotion of aerial agility.

The F6F Hellcat proved itself a prodigiously capable aircraft after it began to enter service with fleet squadrons in January 1943, and is credited with the destruction of 4,947 of the 6,477 Japanese aircraft brought down by US naval aviators in World War II. But even as the F6F was beginning to develop its definitive shape on the drawing boards at the Grumman factory at Bethpage on Long Island in New York state, thought was being given to a successor, or rather companion, of somewhat different mould. Early experience

Altogether different in concept to the F8F, the Grumman F7F Tigercat was the US Navy's first twin-engine fighter and the first carrierborne aircraft with tricycle landing gear.

with the A6M fighter had already revealed the considerably inferior performance of the F4F at low to medium altitudes, and also the American fighter's relative lack of aerial agility. It seemed likely, moreover, that as the war progressed, the Japanese would introduce into widespread service A6M successors with comparable agility, better protection and superior performance, which might therefore eclipse the F6F as a conventional fighter and so open the way for attacks on US carriers by the Imperial Japanese Navy's formidable attack aircraft (dive-bombers, level bombers and torpedo-bombers). What was needed, therefore, was a carrier-borne interceptor fighter in which all was subordinated to rapid take-off from a short run (thereby suiting the aircraft to all types of US aircraft-carrier in service, building or proposed), phenomenal climb rate, high speed, and excellent manoeuvrability in the Japanese fighters' chosen arena at low and medium altitudes. What the Americans needed, in fact, was a type now known as the air superiority fighter, combining the aerodynamic cleanliness and light structure weight of Japanese fighters (for climb rate and agility) with the firepower and strength of the F4F and F6F (for a powerful combat advantage over the Japanese fighters). It is worth noting that by the time the concept was formally defined in early 1943, the F6F was already in service as the US Navy's medium-range multi-role fighter, and the new F7F Tigercat twin-engined fighter was under construction for prototype trials. The Tigercat offered the possibility of exceptional performance coupled with long range and formidable armament for operation from the US Navy's new 45,000-ton (45,720-tonne) 'Midway' class fleet carriers, and the new interceptor would

A highly unusual structural feature of the F8F was the provision of Safety Wing Tips. These were designed to break off cleanly at high g loadings to maximise the survival chances of the rest of the craft.

complete a three-aircraft fighter team that would make the US Navy virtually invincible in the air.

The task of developing the new Grumman G-58 fighter was entrusted to the company's chief engineer, William 'Bill' Schwendler, and basic parameters proposed to and accepted by the US Navy's Bureau of Aeronautics were for an aircraft comparable in size with the F4F (and retaining the same NACA 230 series aerofoil section used in the F4F and F6F), but with rates of climb and roll twice those of the F4F, and with a maximum level speed some 50 mph (80 km/h) higher than that of the F4F. As can readily be imagined, the design task was akin to squeezing a quart into a pint pot, but with the design team's experience with the Wildcat and the Hellcat it was not an impossible task. Fixed armament was reduced from six 0.5-in (12.7-mm) machine-guns with 400 rounds per gun to four 0.5-in (12.7-mm) guns with 300 rounds per gun, which effected a considerable saving in armament and associated structure weight while providing firepower deemed more than adequate to deal with lightly constructed Japanese

aircraft. Pilot protection was planned as being comparable with that of the F6F, whose F6F-3 and F6F-5 versions had included 212 lb (96.16 kg) and 242 lb (109.77 kg) of armour respectively: in the event the F8F included 169 lb (76.66 kg) of armour protection. The arrangement of the retractable tailwheel-type landing gear was altered so that the wide-track main units retracted inwards, rather than to the rear as was the case on the F6F. As much of the F6F's design and structure as possible were carried over to the new fighter, though a considerable difference was the use of thicker skins in conjunction with spot welding and flush riveting to maintain strength while producing a considerably smoother finish for the purposes of drag reduction.

Another feature introduced on the G-58 design was the so-called 'Safety Wing Tip', in an effort to reduce the disastrous results of structural failure in the wing during high-g combat manoeuvres. Schwendler and his team rightly reckoned that if

An admirable fighter-bomber, the F6F had operational failings in that it was large and of indifferent performance at low and medium altitudes.

structural failure were to occur, it would be better that this should occur at a predetermined point, in this instance 3 ft (0.91 m) from each wingtip. At this point, just outboard of the central hinge for the aileron, the wing was designed to fail should the structure be subjected to loads well in excess of the designed 9-g maximum design load. The separation of the wingtip and outboard portion of the aileron would therefore reduce the load on the remaining portion of the wing and leave just enough aileron for lateral control. A useful corollary of this factor was the ability to lighten the inboard wing structure, which did not have to cope with load factors from a full-span wing. To ensure that no asymmetrical effects accrued from the loss of just one wingtip, explosive bolts were built into the system so that the separation of either wingtip would be accompanied by the loss of the other.

The intended powerplant was the excellent Pratt & Whitney R-2800 Double Wasp, one of the classic reciprocating engines of all time, and already a formidable performer in the F6F and a number of other US combat aircraft. The whole design of the G-58 was tailored round this engine, for the designers rightly appreciated that the combination of minimum aircraft round

maximum engine would go a long way towards ensuring the attainment of the difficult performance parameters envisaged. It is worth digressing slightly, therefore, to detail some of the important facts about the mighty Double Wasp, an 18-cylinder air-cooled radial engine with its cylinders arranged in two nine-cylinder rows and rated at powers in the order of 2,000 hp (1491 kW) or more. In its basic form the R-2800 had a swept volume of 2,804 cu in (45949 cc, or 45.949 litres), a bore of 5.75 in (14.605 cm) and a stroke of 6 in (15.24 cm). The overall weight of the R-2800 was some 2,360 lb (1070.5 kg), and though the type developed considerably less horse-power per square inch of piston area than contemporary inline engines, it was conversely less weighty than these liquid-cooled engines, and had the added advantages of compact overall dimensions, less vulnerability to combat damage because of the absence of a cooling system, and a smaller number of parts. This last was particularly important for carrier-borne aircraft as it reduced the necessary spares holding needs of the parent ship and all the support vessels in the fleet train that made possible extended and long-range combat operations in the Pacific Ocean during World War II.

The version of the R-2800

originally intended for the G-58 was the Double Wasp Series 'E' with a fully variable-speed supercharger (in service terminology the R-2800-30 series), but delays with this highly flexible powerplant meant that early aircraft were fitted with the Double Wasp Series 'C' with a two-speed supercharger (in service terminology the R-2800-20 series). Both series were fitted with water-injection capability (indicated by a W suffix in the service designation); this cooled the fuel/air mixture before it entered the cylinders and so delayed detonation by a considerable margin to permit short-term boosts of power.

The Grumman design team began the process of final definition at about the same time that the F6F-3 Hellcat was entering operational service, and later in 1943 the G-58 design was offered to the Bureau of Aeronautics. Grumman had an excellent 'track record' with its naval aircraft, and many of the more senior staff officers in the Bureau of Aeronautics remembered with fondness and appreciation the excellent Grumman aircraft they had flown in the earlier part of the 1930s. It was with little difficulty and minimum change that the G-58 concept was accepted by the US Navy with the basic designation F8F and the name Bearcat. On 27 November 1943 Grumman received a letter of intent for two XF8F-1 prototypes (one to be powered by the Double Wasp Series 'C' and the other by the Double Wasp Series 'E' engine) together with the necessary priority certificates for the building of the aircraft under wartime conditions of production allocation. The task facing Grumman was formidable, but so was the company's reaction.

# Prototypes

The two XF8F-1 prototypes ordered from Grumman on 27 November 1943 were allocated the Bureau of Aeronautics' serial numbers (BuNos) 90460 and 90461, and Grumman pushed through their construction with almost incredible rapidity. The US Navy authorities had already been astounded by the speed with which the F6F Hellcat had been rushed into service (ordered on 30 June 1940, first flown on 26 June 1942 in prototype form and on 30 July 1942 in production form, and first delivered to fleet squadrons on 16 January 1943); but they had a greater shock in store for them with the F8F Bearcat which, as indicated above, was ordered on 27 November 1943, first flown in prototype form on 21 August 1944 and first delivered to an operational unit on 21 May 1945. Thus the Hellcat had been brought into service in under 31 months, while the comparable period for the Bearcat was only 18 months. The process was much speeded by the fact that the Bureau of Aeronautics demanded no full-scale mock-up, but rather mock-ups of two primary sections of the airframe, namely the powerplant installation (inspected and approved in March 1944) and the cockpit section (inspected and approved in January 1944). In April 1944 it was decided to use Series 'C' engines in both prototypes because of delays in Series 'E' engines.

The first XF8F-1 was ready for its initial flight trials just over nine months after the issue of the letter of intent, and a company test pilot took BuNo 90460 into the air for the first time on 31 August 1944. By this time the threat of the Imperial Japanese Navy's air arm had paled into insignificance with the loss of all its main aircraft-carriers, though others were known to be under trial and under construction. Just as importantly, the new generation that the Bearcat had been designed to counter had failed to materialize in any significant numbers, and the high-quality combat-experienced aircrew who had made Japanese aircraft so effective in 1941 and 1942 had by now been decimated, their replacements being wholly inadequate in terms of experience and basic capability thanks to the inadequacy of the Japanese aircrew training programme. The war still continued, however, and it was conceivable that the Japanese could make a resurgence, so the programme for the Bearcat was pushed ahead with all speed.

Hall and other Grumman test pilots put the first XF8F-1 through a rapid series of tests so that the aircraft could participate in the Joint Fighter Conference programme to be held during October 1944 at the Naval Air Test Center at Patuxent River, Maryland. There were few major problems during these initial manufacturer's trials, and though a number of typical teething problems cropped up these were eliminated without too much difficulty. There was little doubt that the new aircraft would meet or exceed all its design parameters, so considerable effort went into the development of this basic model as a combat aircraft. The two major engineering and design problems were concerned with the extension/retraction cycle of the main landing gear units and with insufficient stability in the longitudinal plane. The former was solved by improvements in a number of components, and the latter was remedied by a 1-ft (0.305-m) extension of tailplane span. Other modifications were carried out to the internal fuel tank under the pilot's seat: this had been specified with a capacity of 150 US gal (567.8 litres) but in fact had a volume of 162 US gal (613.25 litres); after initial flight trials this capacity was boosted to 175 US gal (662.45 litres) as there was room under the seat, and the initial production Bearcats featured a further increase in fuel capacity

The XF8F-1 shows off the Bearcat's uncompromised lines, with everything tailored to the maximum interceptor performance.

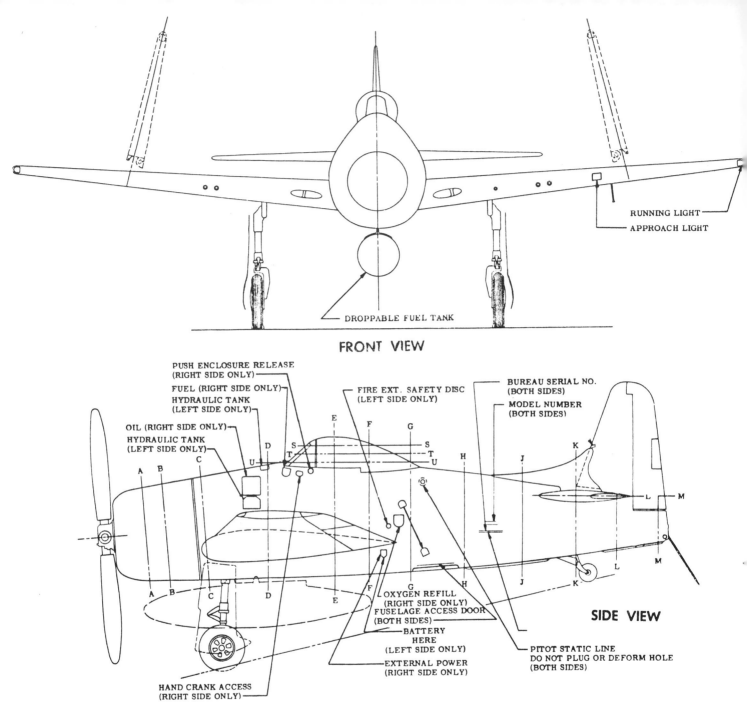

RUNNING LIGHT
APPROACH LIGHT
DROPPABLE FUEL TANK

**FRONT VIEW**

PUSH ENCLOSURE RELEASE
(RIGHT SIDE ONLY)
FUEL (RIGHT SIDE ONLY)
HYDRAULIC TANK
(LEFT SIDE ONLY)
FIRE EXT. SAFETY DISC
(LEFT SIDE ONLY)
BUREAU SERIAL NO.
(BOTH SIDES)
MODEL NUMBER
(BOTH SIDES)
OIL (RIGHT SIDE ONLY)
HYDRAULIC TANK
(LEFT SIDE ONLY)

OXYGEN REFILL
(RIGHT SIDE ONLY)
FUSELAGE ACCESS DOOR
(BOTH SIDES)
BATTERY
HERE
(LEFT SIDE ONLY)
EXTERNAL POWER
(RIGHT SIDE ONLY)
PITOT STATIC LINE
DO NOT PLUG OR DEFORM HOLE
(BOTH SIDES)
HAND CRANK ACCESS
(RIGHT SIDE ONLY)

**SIDE VIEW**

to 183 US gal (692.75 litres) without significant alteration to the basic fuel tank assembly. This increase of more than 20 per cent in basic internal fuel capacity was clearly a marked tactical advantage, and was carried out with no disruption of the flight test programme, and without degradation of the aircraft's first-class performance. The other tactical development of this period was the improvement of the underwing stores capability. Though the type had no real need for such weapons in its primary interceptor role, it had

been felt from an early stage in the G-58 programme that a secondary capability in the fighter-bomber role could be only to the good, and hardpoints had been provided under the wings inboard of the wing-fold line. During the manufacturer's trials this capability was enhanced, and the XF8F-1 was soon tested with two 1,000-lb (454-kg) and four 250-lb (113-kg) bombs under the wings.

The powerplant of this XF8F-1 was an R-2800-22W radial rated at 2,100 hp (1566 kW) at 2,800 rpm for take-off and at

*Top:* The frontal aspect of the F8F is dominated by the very considerable diameter of the massive radial powerplant. *Above:* The side view of the F8F. *Right:* The top view of the Bearcat shows off the comparatively large wing and the relatively large control surfaces.

1,600 hp (1193 kW) at an altitude of 16,000 ft (4875 m). This power was delivered to a massive four-blade propeller made by Aeroproducts and possessing a diameter of 12 ft 7 in (3.83 m). The diameter of the propeller, which was fully necessary to absorb the power of the R-2800 engine, was one of the reasons for the problems with the Bearcat's landing gear, whose legs had to be long to provide adequate clearance at the nose for the propeller.

In June 1944 the original contract for two prototypes had been amended to include a further 23 aircraft (the designations XF8F-1 and F8F-1 are both to be found in official documentation relating to these aircraft, BuNos 90437 to 90459) and the tooling necessary to implement a production rate of 100 aircraft per month. It was planned that the first of the additional 23 aircraft would become available for the flight-test programme in December 1944, complementing the prototypes scheduled to fly in August and November 1944 respectively. It was also decided that at least one of this 23-aircraft additional batch should have the Series 'E' engine, which was scheduled for availability in March 1945 under the service designation R-2800-30W with water injection. Just before the first XF8F-1 moved to the Naval Air Test Center at Patuxent River, Grumman received its first true production contract for the F8F-1 Bearcat initial service model on 6 October 1944: the US Navy contracted for 2,023 aircraft (the 23 service-test aircraft above being transferred to this batch) and specified a monthly production rate of 100 aircraft to be achieved by June 1945. This ambitious programme was boosted further on 5 February 1945 when the Eastern Aircraft Division of General Motors was weaned from its own XF2M-1 design (for larger carriers and with R-1820 engine) and brought into the scheme with an order for 1,876 aircraft essentially similar to the F8F-1 but designated F3M-1 and powered by R-2800-34WR or R-2800-40 engines. The F8F and F3M were slated to supersede the F6F

in production entirely by January 1946.

The XF8F-1 made a very considerable impact during the Joint Fighter Conference, where it was flown by test pilots, service pilots and manufacturers' pilots to almost universal acclaim for its spritely handling and excellent performance. Performance figures returned at this time for the XF8F-1 with empty and normal loaded weights of 6,733 lb (3054 kg) and 8,788 lb (3986 kg) included maximum speeds of 393 mph (632 km/h) at sea level and of 424 mph (682 km/h) at 17,300 ft (5275 m),

and an initial climb rate of 4,800 ft (1463 m) per minute. These figures all relate to the XF8F-1 in clean condition and at combat power.

The results of the Joint Fighter Conference confirmed the universal acceptance of the Bearcat as the best fighter (land, or carrier-based) for operations below 25,000 ft (7620 m) and potentially the best carrier-based fighter of all those present, allowance being given to land-base aircraft for carrier equipment. One of the points most praised was Grumman's move, with Bureau of Aeronautics

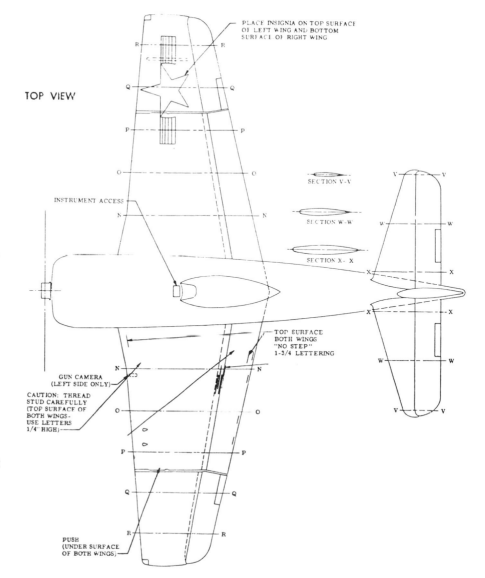

*Above:* BuNo 90456 was built as an F8F-1 but modified by the NAMU as the prototype of the F8F-1D drone-controller aircraft with special avionics.

support, against the trend for ever larger and ever heavier combat aircraft. There were quibbles with the Bearcat, which centered on the small cockpit (with the seat mounted on a rearward extension of the powerplant assembly), a relative lack of directional stability, and the limited trim possible in the lateral and longitudinal planes (the latter was especially notable during the landing regime).

Limited US Navy evaluation of the Bearcat had been undertaken during the Joint Fighter Conference, this including preliminary gun-firing trials, but the prototype then moved into the naval evaluation proper, where a number of small problems and snags were encountered and quite quickly remedied as the manufacturer had already anticipated them. Typical of these were the difficulties with lateral trim and directional stability, the

unreliable operation of the airspeed indicator system, and the tactical desirability of faster landing gear retraction operation, which was also to be possible at higher airspeeds. Some adverse comment about the XF8F-1's relatively light fixed armament had been passed at the Joint Fighter Conference, and this was reflected in a US Navy request at this time that Grumman should investigate the possibility of a six-gun primary armament, though this proved impractical because of limitations on the aft movement of the aircraft's centre of gravity. The aircraft was also tested with a Hamilton Standard Superhydromatic propeller, which proved comparable with the Aeroproducts unit but no better. It was decided to standardize the Aeroproducts propeller as there were doubts about the availability of the Hamilton Standard unit. The

sense of this decision was confirmed by a study of vibration stress carried out by Aeroproducts: this confirmed that propeller-associated stresses were well below known fatigue limits, and the combination of the Aeroproducts propeller and R-2800-34W engine was cleared.

*Right above and below:* Construction number D-1227, this Grumman F8F-2 Bearcat was built for the US Navy with the serial 122674 but was too late for World War II. It then served with the French Armée de l'Air in Indo-China, and is now a prized possession of the Texas-based Confederate Air Force with the civil registration N7825C.

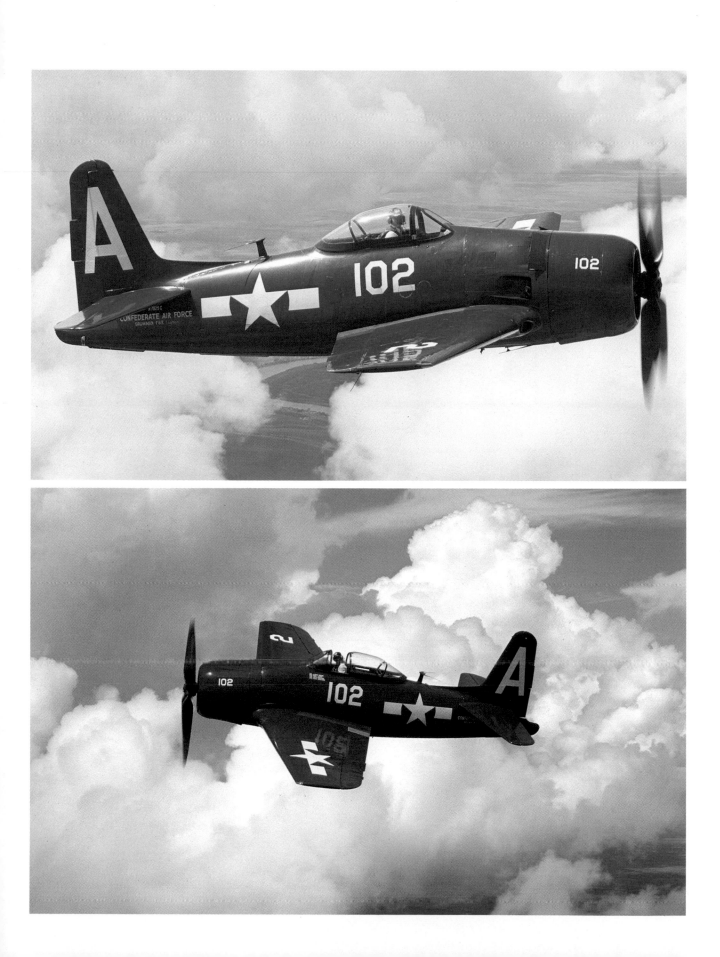

*Right:* An F8F-1 Bearcat in the markings of the Royal Thai Air Force's 1st Fighter-Bomber Wing shows off the stalky look of the type in ground configuration. The longthy main landing gear legs were necessary to provide clearance for the 151-in (3.835-m) diameter four-blade Aeroproducts propeller.

*Below:* A trio of US Navy F8F-1 Bearcats poses for the camera. Part of the principal 747-aircraft production run, these machines sport the national marking adopted in 1947.

*Above:* This F8F-2 Bearcat carries the 'P' fin code that confirms its allocation to the US Navy Reserve base at Denver, Colorado. Well displayed also are the short moment arms and large control surfaces that helped make the Bearcat so formidably agile in the air-to-air combat role.

*Above right:* Seen in the landing regime, the Denver-based F8F-2 shows off its powerful flaps and tall vertical tail, the latter vital for adequate directional control even at high angles of attack.

*Right:* The only Bearcat built for the civil market was the sole G-58A built for Alford Williams, who christened his short-lived aircraft *Gulfhawk 4.*

*Above left:* The F8F-2 was admirably compact, its folded dimensions including a span of 23 ft 3 in (7.09 m) and a height of 13 ft 8 in (4.17 m) with a propeller blade vertical.
*Below left:* The whole powerplant installation of the Bearcat series was a triumph of clean and compact design for minimum drag and maximum performance.

*Above:* In classic form, the Bearcat was finished in 'midnite' blue overall, with national markings, white unit/base markings and (usually) a coloured rear fuselage band.

*Below:* Though tall (and thus inhibitive of the pilot's forward vision), the landing gear of the Bearcat was sturdy and, with a track of 12 ft (3.66 m), well suited to carrier operations.

The naval evaluation of the type was much speeded by the availability of the second XF8F-1, which was first flown on 2 December 1944 by Pat Gallo, a Grumman test pilot. This aircraft, BuNo 90461, was used for simulated carrier landings (with arrester gear) at Philadelphia, and was distinguishable from BuNo 90460 by its small dorsal fin, introduced to cure the directional stability problem and used on all subsequent Bearcat aircraft. As BuNo 90461 underwent its trials at Philadelphia,

*Opposite page, top:* Increasing interest in historic aircraft had led to a useful revival in the restoration field. This F8F-2 is typical of the type, and was restored to pristine condition by 1975.

*Opposite page, bottom:* In beautiful condition at the Naval Air Station, Patuxent River, Md is seen this F8F-1 restored in the markings of the Royal Thai Air Force's 1st Fighter-Bomber Wing.

*Below:* A factory-fresh F8F-1 shows off the type's pristine condition. Clearly displayed are the small strip-like ventral fins fore and aft of the tailwheel unit.

BuNo 90460 was shifted to the Langley Field facility of the National Advisory Committee for Aeronautics for full-scale wind tunnel tests. These revealed no new problems.

Meanwhile, Grumman had been pressing ahead with the batch of 23 service-test aircraft, by now absorbed into the first production batch: BuNo 90437 was completed on 1 January 1945, BuNo 90438 before the end of the month and BuNo 90439 during February. This marked a critical point in the history of the Bearcat, for BuNo 90439 was the last aircraft of the series to be built in Grumman's experimental shop, BuNo 90440 and its successors coming off the main production line. BuNo 90440 can thus be considered the pilot for production assembly, and was flight tested during February 1945.

At this stage in the programme, with production under way, problems began to emerge as

earlier aircraft were evaluated more thoroughly than had hitherto been possible. The main difficulty was with the range of the Bearcat, established as a nominal 600 miles (966 km) during the initial trials with the first XF8F-1 (BuNo 90460). But during January 1945 exhaustive range trials were undertaken with BuNo 90461, the US Navy having realized that, even though the Bearcat was designed as a short-range interceptor, range performance was essential for adequate and safe operations in the vastnesses of the Pacific Ocean, the theatre for which the Bearcat was intended. These trials of January 1945 were thus very disappointing, for the auto-lean control used for long-range cruise at low power was adversely affected by the idle needle to produce too rich a fuel/air mixture with disastrous effects on range. The problem was entrusted to the Pratt & Whitney team, who

*Left:* The F8F-2 was a relatively 'short-legged' fighter as a result of the original requirement for a fast-climbing close-range interceptor, and was generally operated with a jettisonable tank under the fuselage for an extra 150 US gal (568 litres) of fuel.

*Below left:* The cowling and cooling arrangements for the big R-2800 radial of the Bearcat series were both compact and aerodynamically efficient. Also notable on this view of an F8F-2 are the barrels and muzzles of the four 20-mm cannon.

*Right:* Seen before a test flight in September 1944, the XF8F-1 reveals the Bearcat's great height in the 'gear down' configuration to provide adequate clearance for the Aeroproducts four-blade propeller.

*Below:* Though conceived as an interceptor, the Bearcat was rightly fitted from the outset with underwing provision for drop-tanks or ordnance.

A Bearcat in its elements, with an F8F-1 spotted on the flightdeck of USS *Charger*, a 'Long Island' class escort carrier. It was from such small platforms that the Bearcat was designed to deliver high-performance air defence.

came up with a manually operated lean control that did the trick, albeit at the expense of fouled spark plugs. This in turn required another fix. Another problem with the powerplant, parallel to but unconnected with the range factor, was met with the carburation and ignition. This proved a more complex difficulty, and was not finally solved until after the Bearcat's entry into service; the problem and its solution are treated more fully below.

The availability of additional aircraft also permitted the evaluation of underwing stores combinations. Mixes that were cleared for the F8F-1 included a centreline 150-US gal (567.8-litre) drop tank and two underwing 1,000-lb (454-kg) bombs; a centreline 150-US gal (567.8-litre) drop tank and two under-

wing 100-US gal (378.5-litre) drop tanks; one centreline 150-US gal (567.8-litre) drop tank and two underwing Mk 1 gun-pods, each with two 0.5-in (12.7-mm) machine-guns; two underwing 11.75-in (298-mm) 'Tiny Tim' unguided rockets; and the combinations already mentioned above. Another armament possibility under active investigation at the beginning of 1945 was the replacement of the four machine-guns in the wings by four 20-mm cannon. The F8F-1 was still considered primarily as an interceptor, but the waning of Japanese air opposition and the very cap-abilities of the aircraft promoted the type's development as a fighter-bomber with the full range of US Navy air-to-surface weapons.

A date of signal importance for the Bearcat was 17 February 1945, for on this day the type made its first landings on and take-offs from an aircraft carrier, the aircraft in question being BuNo 90438 that had under-

taken most of the armament trials mentioned above. Flown by Lieutenant Commander Bottomley and Lieutenant Commander Elder from the Naval Air Station Mustin Field at Philadelphia, Pennsylvania, the aircraft made a total of nine landings and nine take-offs from the escort carrier USS *Charger* (CVE-30). These presented no problems whatsoever in terms of performance or deck handling, and it was clear that so success-ful a trial aboard a 'baby flat-top' could only augur well for operations aboard the US Navy's light aircraft carriers and fleet aircraft carriers.

BuNo 90438 was then turned over to the Board of Inspection and Survey at NAS Mustin Field for the completion of arrester and catapult trials. No major difficulties were met, though the BIS made the strong recom-mendation that the Bearcat should not be operated with asymmetric underwing loads, this being a legacy of the directional instability problem

countered by the addition of the dorsal fillet on the second and subsequent Bearcats. The BIS trials continued throughout March and April 1945 at the Naval Air Test Center: BuNo 90460 was flown in armament trials (crashing on 26 February and being replaced by BuNo 90440 in late March for continued armament trials connected with bomb and rocket installations), BuNo 90439 was used for fuel consumption tests, BuNo 90441 was used for demonstrations after BuNo 90437 had been damaged in structural build-up tests and relegated to static-airframe test duties at Bethpage, BuNo 90444 began the Bearcat's acceptance trials, and BuNo 90442 was used for the type's service tests. These last were pushed through at an accelerated pace facilitated by the allocation of another aircraft (BuNo 90477) to the programme in May 1945. Again a number of small problems were encountered, which is hardly surprising given the speed with which the entire

programme had been implemented: the flaps proved prone to partial retraction during the approach phase; the stick forces were too light at high speed; lateral trim was ineffective throughout the Bearcat's speed range; and other similar problems such as brake failures, oil leaks, hydraulic-fluid leaks and continued engine difficulties.

*Above:* Powerful controls and compact overall dimensions made the F8F-1 a formidable dogfighter, well able to best other legendary combat aircraft of World War II.

*Below:* Service evaluation at the Naval Air Test Center did much to develop the F8F-1 into a reliable and effective combat aircraft in a remarkably short time.

Looking sleek and menacing over a wintry landscape, the F8F-1 began delivery to the US Navy in May 1945, the first operational unit being VF-19.

By the end of May 1945 Grumman had effected a number of fixes, including a bobweight in the elevator system to cure the lightness in the manoeuvring-force gradient, exhaust deflector plates on the wing roots, a reduction in fin offset from 2° to 1.5°, and installation of dive-recovery flaps.

Two other early-production F8F-1s should also be mentioned at this point: BuNo 90446 was allocated to the Naval Air Test Center for electronic trials, and BuNo 90461 was handed over to NACA at Langley Field for a thorough and unpartisan evaluation of the Bearcat's flight characteristics. By this time the Bearcat was ready for its service debut, and much was expected of it. Germany had surrendered earlier in May 1945, and the only surviving enemy for the US Navy was the Japanese, who were expected to fight to the bitter end. Against this eventuality the Americans planned to invade the Japanese home islands in two massive amphibious operations, Operation 'Olympic' scheduled for November 1945 to put the US 6th Army ashore on Kyushu Island in the south of Japan, and Operation 'Coronet' slated for March 1946 with the aim of hurling the US 1st and 8th Armies ashore to the north and south of Tokyo respectively on Honshu Island. It was anticipated that the Bearcat would play a key part in these operations, preventing the attacks of Japanese conventional and *kamikaze* aircraft on the huge American invasion fleets and supporting the ground forces as they slogged inland.

The importance of the Bearcat programme is confirmed by Grumman's receipt in April 1945 of an order for an additional 2,000 Bearcats.

# Into Service

Despite all the modifications and service 'extras' loaded onto the type, the production F8F-1 Bearcat was little different from the XF8F-1 prototype. Weight had inevitably grown: the F8F-1 turned the scales at 7,070 lb (3207 kg) empty, 9,386 lb (4257 kg) normal loaded and 12,947 lb (5872 kg) maximum loaded. But performance was maintained at little below the levels of the XF8F-1 by the adoption of the R-2800-34W engine, which had the same take-off rating as the R-2800-22W used in the XF8F-1 but which was capable of delivering combat powers of 2,750 hp (2051 kW) at sea level, 2,450 hp (1827 kW) at 9,600 ft (2925 m) and 1,850 hp (1380 kW) at 15,500 ft (4725 m). With this engine the F8F-1 turned in maximum speeds ranging from 421 mph (678 km/h) at sea level to 428 mph (689 km/h) at 18,800 ft (5730 m), while the initial climb rate was 5,610 ft (1710 m) per minute and time to 20,000 ft (6095 m) a mere 4 minutes 54 seconds. Range was still on the low side, and it was generally accepted that the F8F-1 would retain its 150-US gal (567.8-litre) centreline drop tank even in combat, releasing it only when empty.

The aircraft itself was compact and designed to facilitate carrier operations and to provide the pilot with excellent fields of vision. The basic physical dimensions of this illustrious 'Cat' included a span of 35 ft 6 in (10.82 m) reducing to 23 ft 3 in (7.09 m) when folded for carriage stowage, a length of 27 ft 6 in (8.38 m) and a height of 13 ft 8 in (4.17 m) with the tailwheel on the ground and the propeller vertical. Within these overall dimensions the wings had an area of 244 sq ft (22.67 m²)

with a root chord of 115.9 in (2.94 m) tapering to a tip chord of 51.5 in (1.31 m) some 6 in (15.24 cm) inboard of the very tip; of this wing area the slotted flaps accounted for 18.18 sq ft (1.69 m²) and could be drooped through 40°, the Frise-type ailerons with spring tabs and trim tab occupied 15 sq ft (1.39 m²) and the dive-recovery flaps amounted to 1.38 sq ft (0.128 m²). Dihedral was 5.5°. The horizontal tail spanned 15 ft 9 in (4.80 m) and was set at a positive incidence angle of 0.5°; overall area was 52.27 sq ft (4.86 m²) including the elevators and trim tabs' 18.63 sq ft (1.73 m²). The vertical tail was offset at an angle of 1.5° (leading edge to port) and had an overall area of 17.7 sq ft (1.64 m²) including a rudder and tab area of 6.7 sq ft (0.62 m²).

As far back as the leading edge of the wing, the fuselage was occupied by the engine, its rear face against a stainless steel fireproof bulkhead which was pierced for items such as fuel lines, electrical leads, oil-cooler lines and exhaust collector pipes. A ring of large cowling flaps to control cooling air for the radial engine surrounded this rear section of the engine compartment. To the immediate rear of the engine compartment was the accessory compartment containing items such as the engine bearer structure, the induction and oil-cooler air ducts taking air from the inlets in the wing roots, the 16-US gal (60.57-litre) water tank, the 17-US gal (64.35-litre) oil tank, the engine control runs and the hydraulic distribution unit. This compartment ended with a 29.3-lb (13.3-kg) armoured bulkhead forming the forward edge of the cockpit compartment: here sat the pilot on an armoured seat providing 49.4 lb (22.4 kg) of head and back protection, his field of vision from the high-set bubble canopy with bulletproof

windscreen being excellent; the pilot's primary weapon-aiming aid was the Mk 8 Model 6 illuminated reflector gunsight; and under the pilot's seat was the internal fuel tank, a self-sealing unit with a capacity of 183 US gal (692.7 litres). Behind the cockpit section and grouped on the floor of the fuselage was the communications and battery assembly in the rear-fuselage section, which was of typical frame-and-stringer structure with stressed-skin covering as on the rest of the fuselage; this section accommodated the control runs to the tail, and had in its lower rear a compartment for the retractable tailwheel unit. The arrester hook was also retractable, and fitted neatly into the extreme tail, which was completed by the conventional tailplane and vertical surfaces. The wing was also conventional, and built up on the basis of two main and one auxiliary spar with 17 main ribs in each half. At about quarter span were located the two main landing gear units, arranged to retract inwards and be covered fully by doors attached to the main landing gear units and the underside of the fuselage. Outboard of the landing gear units were the Colt-Browning 0.5-in (12.7-mm) machine-guns and their ammunition tanks together with the pylon for external stores on the underside of the wing. Outboard again was the folding mechanism for the outer wing panels. All in all, it was a thoroughly sound and workmanlike structure, very carefully and nicely designed with a view to operational capability and ease of maintenance, and characterized by extreme strength.

The Bearcat began to reach the US Navy as an operational aircraft on 21 May 1945 when Fighting Squadron 19 (VF-19) at the Naval Air Station Santa Rosa in California received the first Bearcats delivered to an operational unit. This squadron,

In their aerial element, F8F-1 Bearcats
from a US Navy escort carrier formate
closely for the camera..

commanded by Lieutenant Commander Joseph G. Smith, was soon in receipt of the last of the 23 service test/initial production aircraft, plus the first machines off the main production run, starting with BuNo 94752. The squadron was immediately caught up in a frantic programme of operational conversion and working-up, but this was delayed by a relative shortage of aircraft (less than half the planned 40 F8F-1s were delivered in May, rising to 48 aircraft in June) because of problems with the installation of the landing gear doors, with the engine and with the hydraulic system. As production began to improve in rate of delivery, VF-19 was able to accelerate its training programme, and further aircraft could be delivered to the Naval Air Test Center at Patuxent River for further trials. These were progressing well, but the pace of operations was also throwing up another spate of relatively minor problems: component failures in the hydraulic system, cracking in the exhaust system, and poor directional stability at high speed when the aircraft was carrying the centreline drop tank. Other trials were conducted with an aerodynamic mock-up of the F8F-1N night-fighter variant, which mounted an AN/APS-19 airborne interception radar in a pod mounted under the starboard wing on the standard stores pylon, and with rocket-firing. The latter was undertaken at the Naval Air Station Inyokern in California. Production of the F8F-1N amounted to 14 conversions, comprising two proto- types and 12 'production' aircraft.

Meanwhile VF-19 had been pressing ahead with the service introduction of the F8F-1, only to run across a major engine problem: a number of pilots reported intermittent cutting-out by the R-2800 radial, and five

pilots suffered total failure, though all of the latter were able to achieve successful dead-stick landings. In part the problem was attributed to pilot inexperience with the engine: cut-out in cruising flight was generally due to the use of too lean a fuel/air mixture, and cut-out after take- off seemed attributable to an inadequate warm-up period. However, the total engine failures and a few of the more significant intermittent failures could not be traced to such a cause, and the problem was eventually found to lie with the fuel-feed valves, and more specifically to leakages in their diaphragms and seals. The squadron was grounded for a short time as these failings were remedied, and by mid-July the Bearcat was again declared airworthy. The training programme was then marred by two fatal accidents, neither of them stemming from the previously experienced engine difficulties. But by the end of the month VF-19 had undertaken successful carrier qualifications aboard the USS *Takanis Bay* (CVE-89).

By the end of July 1945 VF-19 was declared ready for operational deployment, and was embarked on the light carrier USS *Langley* (CVL-27) on 2 August for operations in the western Pacific. The carrier had reached Hawaii, and the squadron was completing its operational work-up aboard the carrier, when news of the end of the war against Japan was received. So the Bearcat was denied its part in the Pacific war despite the magnificent efforts of the Grumman designers and production teams, coupled with the rapid entry of the Bearcat into operational service in the hands of US Navy development and operational personnel. Yet further expansion of the Bearcat force was already under way, and this development was not cancelled immediately with the

end of hostilities. With the embarkation of VF-19 for the operational zone at the beginning of August, the squadron's super- numerary Bearcats were available for the equipment of another squadron, VF-18, whose pilots ferried five of these machines to the Naval Air Station North Island at San Diego, California, on 9 August. The squadron also began to receive new F8F-1 fighters straight from the produc- tion line, the first such machine being delivered on 10 August to allow the squadron to start its work-up programme.

While the crash programme to provide the US Navy with operational Bearcat squadrons was pushing ahead thanks to Grumman's stirling production effort (56 aircraft were delivered in July, dropping to a mere 20 units in August after the impetus in the programme was removed by the end of the war against Japan), evaluation of the Bearcat was still under way by NACA and the Naval Air Test Center, both of whom continued to experience problems with the new fighter. In fact one aircraft was lost to each organization through landing accidents at the beginning of August: NACA's BuNo 90461 and NATC's 90442 were both lost, the former bringing the NACA effort to a temporary halt only after a long- term solution to the Bearcat's directional instability problem had been found: NACA proposed that the vertical tail should be heightened by 16 in (40.64 cm) to provide more positive direc- tional stability. But though NACA was right from the aerodynamic

*Above right:* The tall tail of the F8F series (seen here is an F8F-1B in US Marine Corps markings) was necessary for adequate directional control with under- wing loads at high angles of attack.
*Right:* A keynote of the Bearcat's design was utmost aerodynamic cleanliness consonant with military requirements, and this is readily appreciable on this F8F-1 of the main production run.

point of view, analysis of the suggestion by Grumman structural engineers and stress analysts revealed that such an extension would impose severe stresses on the rear fuselage, and would in fact require the whole of the rear fuselage to be redesigned. As a half-way measure Grumman suggested that significant improvements in directional stability could be achieved by increasing the height of the vertical tail by 12 in (30.48 cm), which would not require the redesign of the rear fuselage, and so save time and effort. This proposal was accepted for incorporation on the improved second production variant, the F8F-2.

In common with other US combat aircraft, the Bearcat suffered a drastic reduction in orders with the end of the war in August 1945. Though the cutback in planned production was not as drastic as with other types, the contracts for Bearcat production were nevertheless savaged: planned Bearcat production had amounted to 5,899 aircraft (4,023 F8F-1s from Grumman and 1,876 F3M-1s from General Motors), but contract trimming at the end of the war reduced this to 769 F8Fs from Grumman. As noted

above, the production rate had dropped drastically in August 1945, and from September of that year a monthly rate of 15 aircraft became the norm. There was no doubt, however, that the US Navy regarded the Bearcat highly, for the reduction in Bearcat contracts was proportionally less than that for other naval fighters. This may seem a little strange given the fact that the F8F-1 had not yet been fully accepted for service, for BuNo 90447 (the second aircraft in the programme) did not complete its 453 hours in the accelerated service trials schedule until the beginning of September, qualifying the original aircraft for full-scale service. However, so many detail changes had been incorporated in the Bearcat as a result of early trials that a second accelerated service trials programme was necessary with an aircraft up to definitive production standard, BuNo 94879, the 151st production article. While generally satisfactory, the report resulting from the accelerated service trials confirmed that although a number of significant improvements had been made, it had to be admitted that the exhaust and hydraulic systems were unsatisfactory; it was even

stated that the unreliability of the hydraulics associated with the landing gear actuation/retraction cycle was so great that extensive use of the emergency system had confirmed its total reliability.

While the accelerated service trials with BuNo 94879 started, a new variant entered the lists when BuNo 94803, the first of 100 F8F-1C fighters, was accepted for flight tests at the Naval Air Test Center. The F8F-1C was a more heavily armed variant, with a fixed armament of four 20-mm cannon with 205 rounds per gun in place of the normal quartet of 0.5-in (12.7-mm) heavy machine-guns. Though achieved with little structural modification, the installation of the four cannon added some 440 lb (200 kg) to the Bearcat's empty weight. Flight trials confirmed that this entailed a slight reduction in performance: maximum speed was lowered by 2.5 mph (4 km/h) and initial climb rate dropped by between 250 and 300 ft (76 and 91 m) per minute. It was nevertheless decided that a proportion of these

*Below, right and below right:* The F8F-2 was a 'product improved' Bearcat, taking advantage of operational experience with the F8F-1 series to produce a better armed and more manageable fighter.

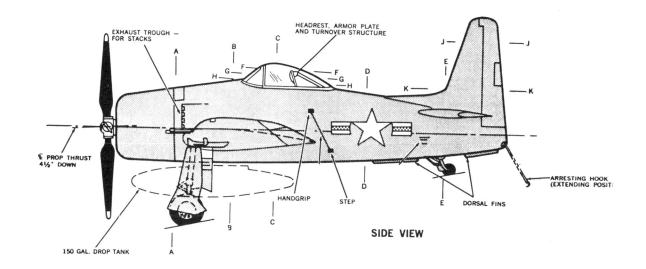

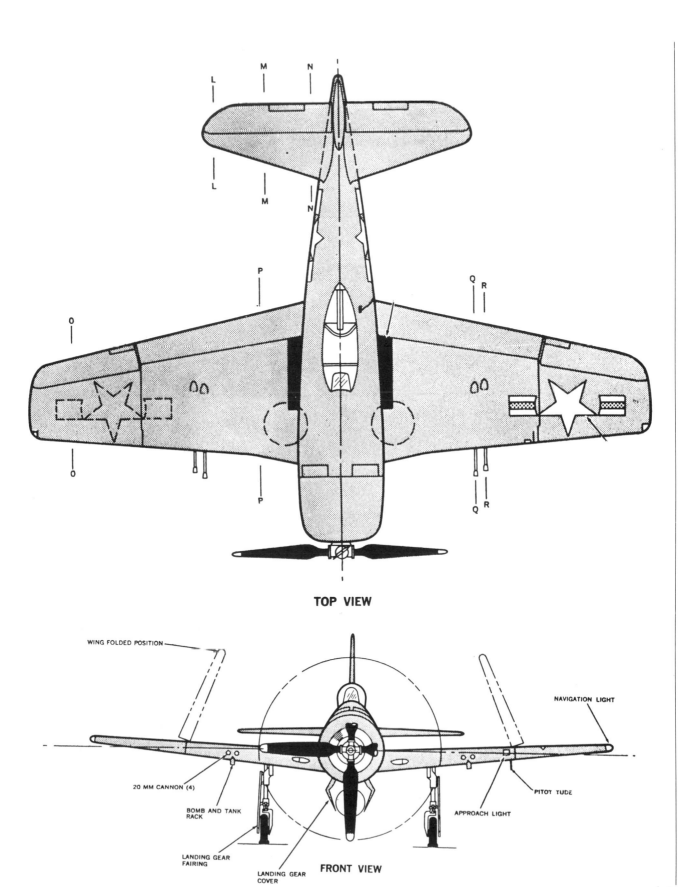

**TOP VIEW**

WING FOLDED POSITION

NAVIGATION LIGHT

20 MM CANNON (4)

PITOT TUDE

BOMB AND TANK RACK

APPROACH LIGHT

LANDING GEAR FAIRING

**FRONT VIEW**

LANDING GEAR COVER

Highly evocative picture of an F8F-2 Bearcat restored to military markings, in this instance 'The Red Rippers' of the US Navy.

*Left:* A F8F-2 in flight. Note the heightened tail and the four 20-mm cannon in the wings.

*Below left:* The introduction of cannon armament meant that the upper surface of the F8F-2's wing had to be bulged to accommodate the breech mechanisms of these considerably more powerful and heavier weapons.

*Below:* Showing the minimum civil markings required by law, this F8F-2 in the markings of VF-41 'The Red Rippers' was originally BuNo 121751, and after a racing career at Reno, Nevada is now part of the 'Flying Tigers' Air Museum and Warbirds Flying School at Paris, Texas.

more powerfully armed fighters would usefully complement the standard F8F-1s, and it was decided to continue with the type as part of the basic F8F-1 production contract. On 27 March 1946 the US Navy decided to abandon the letter C suffix for cannon-armed fighters, and the F8F-1C thereupon became the F8F-1B.

Service squadrons had meanwhile been receiving new Bearcats from the slowed production line, and a new operational deployment scheme had been adopted: the current two squadrons of Carrier Air Group 18 (CVG-18) were to be based on the eastern seaboard of the

continental USA after being shipped from the west coast through the Panama Canal in the USS *Ranger* (CV-4), while the two squadrons of CVG 19 were to remain on the western seaboard with headquarters at the Naval Air Station Alameda, California. It should be noted that although the US Navy was still dedicated to the rapid service introduction of this important fighter, at unit level squadrons found the going very hard as personnel changed rapidly with the swift demobilization of wartime pilots and groundcrew.

Further difficulty was encountered in December 1945, when an F8F-1 was lost together with its pilot during aerobatic manoeuvres. The cause of the crash was impossible to determine with certainty, but the board of inquiry concluded that the probable cause was the separation of only one safety wing tip. At this time the tips had no provision for sympathetic separation with explosives, and it was felt that while one tip might have separated under the designed structural system, the other did not and so caused severe asymmetrical conditions that made the aircraft roll and crash before the pilot could regain control. Grumman had demonstrated that the separation of a single tip was not in itself

The F8F-2 enjoyed only a moderately short but nevertheless impressive career in the US Navy after World War II.

sufficient to cause an uncontrollable roll, but these tests had been undertaken in atypical conditions with a highly experienced test pilot at medium altitude. The solution adopted to this problem was relatively simple: the addition of a detonating cap and prima-cord in each wingtip, the system being wired to ensure that the separation of one tip for aerodynamic reasons would trigger the detonator in the other tip and so weaken the structure that separation would inevitably follow. Later it was decided that as the US Navy was not currently involved in combat, this separation feature was unnecessary and was therefore removed, the addition of extra rivets removing the weak point.

In the spring of 1946 the obsolescence of the Bearcat as a first-line fighter was fully revealed. Trials were undertaken at the Naval Air Test Center

between a standard F8F-1 and a Lockheed P-80 Shooting Star turbojet-powered fighter being used for evaluation purposes. Both pilots were combat veterans and highly experienced airmen, but the conclusion was unambiguous: the Bearcat pilot was unable to hold the Shooting Star in his sights long enough even for a snap burst, the jet aircraft could outfly the piston-engined machine under all combat conditions, and the tactical initiative lay exclusively with the jet aircraft. This was no reflection on the Bearcat as such, but rather an indication of the pace with which the transition to a new era in combat aircraft was proceeding: the piston-engined fighter was now totally outclassed.

An indication of the Bearcat's capabilities in its own genre is provided by the results of a competition between an F8F-1 and a North American P-51D

An F8F-2 is swayed up from the quayside at Norfolk, Virginia to USS *Franklin D. Roosevelt* before Atlantic Fleet exercises in the Caribbean. Such exercises confirmed that the Bearcat had been rendered obsolescent by early jet fighters in the pure interception role.

Mustang, regarded by many as the supreme land-based fighter of World War II. In this competition the two aircraft lined up side-by-side on the runway were instructed to release their brakes simultaneously: by the time the Mustang had taken off, retracted its landing gear and pulled up its flaps, the Bearcat had already made two firing passes on it, and thereafter the Mustang pilot could not cope with the Bearcat at low and medium altitudes. The US Navy was fully aware of the fact that piston-engined fighters were now obsolescent as a breed, but pending the delivery of fully-fledged naval fighters of the type it was decided to maintain the Bearcat and Vought F4U Corsair

This photograph was taken on 5 June
1950 to commemorate the retirement of
the F6F-5 as the US Navy's advanced
trainer in favour of the F8F-2, seen here
with practice bomb racks.

in production and service as first-line fighters.

Thus in 1946 production increased to about 30 aircraft per month, about one in four of each month's total being a cannon-armed fighter. During the year another four US Navy squadrons transitioned to the type, and by the end of the year nine squadrons were operational with the F8F-1: these included VF-18, VBF-18, VF-19, VBF-19, VF-20, VBF-20, VF-81 and VBF-82. During the year the deliveries of production aircraft switched to a revised-standard F8F-1 from the 251st aircraft onwards: these machines had the modified safety wing tips, deflectors on the gun ejector chutes, and steel strips along the leading edges of the tailplane to prevent damage from spent cartridge cases. Grumman had also modified BuNo 94873 as the prototype of the improved

F8F-2 series with the taller tail and the Series 'E' R-2800-30W engine, and this was also evaluated by the Naval Air Test Center and by NACA, proving generally satisfactory though it was also decided by November 1946 to add the dorsal fillet of the F8F-1 series to production F8F-2 aircraft, which were to be built from 1947 under the terms of a 126-aircraft contract issued in August 1946. The year also saw the debut of the Bearcat as the mount of the US Navy's crack aerobatic display team, the 'Blue Angels', and the type also captured the imagination of the public after some astounding climb demonstrations during the 1946 National Air Races at Reno, Nevada.

In the event, production of the F8F-2 was delayed until 1948, and from the middle to the end of 1947 production of Bearcats was

of the F8F-1B model with four cannon. By the end of the year some 19 first-line US Navy fighter squadrons were operational with the F8F-1 while another four squadrons fielded the F8F-1B variant.

During 1947 Grumman also produced the only two Bearcats not built against US Navy orders.

*Opposite page:* F8F-2 Bearcats from the USS *Princeton,* a light carrier, pose for the camera in a stepped-up echelon starboard formation.
*Below:* For a period the US Navy's great aerobatic team, 'The Blue Angels', was equipped with the F8F-1. This photograph, taken in 1946, shows the distinctive 'Midnite Blue' finish with light leading-edge stripes, and the unusual fin markings comprising just the number of each aircraft within the team.

*Below:* The only Bearcat built for
a civilian customer was the G-58A
'Gulfhawk 4' produced to the order of
Major Alford 'Al' Williams and first flown
on 23 July 1947. This short-lived aircraft
was modelled on the F8F-1 and was lost
in a landing accident.

*Left:* The company-owned Bearcat flown
by Rodger Kahn.

The first of these was the G-58A equivalent of an F8F-1 produced for Major Alford 'Al' Williams, a notable exponent of Grumman fighters' manoeuvrability in the 1930s. Named *Gulfhawk 4*, the G-58A was stripped of military equipment (guns, armour and the like), and first took to the air in June 1947. It was painted in a resplendent colour scheme: orange fuselage with blue trim, and white/orange ray motif on the upper and lower surfaces of the flying surfaces. The career of

the *Gulfhawk 4* was short, the aircraft being severely damaged in a landing accident and given up by Williams. The other civil Bearcat was a company-owned demonstrator combining the powerplant of the F8F-1 with the airframe of the F8F-2 series. The aircraft was built from spare parts, and was flown by Rodger Kahn to tour US Navy air stations at which Bearcat operational squadrons were based.

The 'Gulfhawk 4' was powered by the civil version of the R-2800, the Pratt & Whitney Double Wasp 'C' series radial.

# Final Developments

Production of the F8F-1B variant of the Bearcat was phased out at the beginning of 1948, and the improved F8F-2 model then started to come off the lines at Bethpage. First came two 'production pilot' conversions from F8F-1 standard, namely BuNos 95049 and 95330, and then came the first of 126 production aircraft with the taller tail and R-2800-30W engine. Armament was identical with that of the F8F-1B, and the only equipment modification was the addition of a radio altimeter. Because of the improved power-plant, some local modifications had to be made to the basic structure of the fuselage, and while the F8F-2 was inferior to the F8F-1 in terms of low-level performance, high-altitude cap-abilities (especially speed and service ceiling) were improved quite usefully. This in fact was a sensible trade-off, for the conditions of the late 1940s were shifting away from the norms of the Pacific war to which the Bearcat had been designed: the primary air threat to US Navy ships was now seen as jet bombers operating at higher speeds and greater altitudes.

Production of the F8F-2 continued up to May 1949, when the line was finally closed. Production amounted to 365 aircraft of the F8F-2 series, this total including 12 F8F-2N night-fighters (with the underwing podded AN/APS-19 airborne interception radar and a radar scope in the centre of the instrument panel) and 60 F8F-2P reconnaissance aircraft (with a camera installation aft of the cockpit in the lower fuselage and wing armament reduced to two 20-mm cannon).

By the time production of the Bearcat was completed, there were 24 first-line squadrons equipped with the type, 12 having the F8F-1 variant and the other 12 the F8F-2 model. There-after the type declined rapidly in numbers as the first truly effective carrierborne jet fighter, the Grumman F9F Panther, began to enter service. By the end of 1950s the Bearcat was no longer in service as a first-line fighter, the relegation of the type to secondary duties being hastened by the outbreak of the Korean War during that year. US Navy analysis showed that

*Above right:* BuNo 95049 was a development machine, this F8F-1B being re-engined with the R-2800-30W as a step towards the definitive F8F-2.
*Right:* F8F-2 Bearcat in civil hands but complete in US Navy markings.

The company-owned Bearcat seen with two later Grumman naval aircraft: nearer the camera is an F9F-8T Cougar, two-seat trainer version of the F9F-8 fighter, while farther from the camera is an F11F-1 Tiger.

NAVY

141750

NAVY

142500

*Right:* The F8F-2P was a reconnaissance fighter variant of the F8F-2, 60 being built with camera installation and only two cannon.
*Below:* An F8F-2P.

the Bearcat lacked the payload/range performance to make it a viable combat aircraft in this arena, and F8F-1s and F8F-2s were soon used only by US Navy Reserve squadrons (up to 1953). The F8F-2Ps had a slightly longer lease of first-line life, remaining in service up to the end of 1952.

But the career of the Bearcat in US Navy service was not yet over, for the type still had a last task to perform as a drone-director aircraft. BuNo 90456 was converted as a prototype for this role by the Naval Air Test Center during 1949, and proved eminently successful. Armament was reduced to two 20-mm cannon, and to balance the weight of the drone-control equipment located in the rear fuselage, ballast was added in the engine compartment. Further trials were carried out by VX 2, and as a result F8F-1s and F8F-2s were converted under the designations F8F-1D and

F8F-2D respectively, remaining in useful service until 1954.

But though the F8F had not tasted combat in the hands of the service that had ordered it, the Bearcat was still destined to see action, though only in the ground-support rather than interceptor role. Under the terms of the Mutual Defense Assistance Program, ex-US Navy Bearcats were in 1951 supplied to the French Armée de l'Air, hotly involved in Indo-China as part of the effort to prevent the Viet Minh movement from making severe nationalist inroads into this cornerstone of the French empire. About 120 Bearcats were supplied to the French, the aircraft being F8F-1s and F8F-1Bs modified under the revised designation F8F-1D and F8F-1DB with different fuel systems. The first of these aircraft were shipped to Saigon, the capital of French Indo-China, and were immediately allocated to Groupe de Chasse I/6 'Corse'. This unit

used the Bearcat for only a short time as it returned to France in September 1951, but the aircraft were handed on to the Groupe de Marche I/8 'Saintonge', which flew more than 1,000 operational sorties with the type before the end of 1951. The Bearcat immediately proved itself a highly capable ground-attack fighter, its agility and high-speed at low level making it possible to deliver ordnance accurately and with minimum interference in the tree- and mountain-studded confines of Indo-China. By the end of 1951 GM I/8 had been complemented by the Groupe de Marche III/6 'Roussillon', which turned its Bearcats over to the Groupe de Chasse II/8 'Langue-doc' before its return to France in February 1952. By 1953 the two Bearcat units had been redesignated I/22 and II/22, and during the year were sup-plemented by another three Bearcat units, namely the Groupe de Chasse I/9 'Limousin', the

Groupe de Chasse II/9 'Auvergne' (the latter being redesignated II/21 in October 1953) and the Groupe de Chasse I/21 'Artois'. The last French unit to operate the Bearcat in Indo-China was a reconnaissance squadron, the Escadrille de Reconnaissance d'Outre-Mer 80, which flew F8F-1DB aircraft equipped with a centreline reconnaissance pod containing cameras. The Bearcat served for about three years in Indo-China, and was universally admired by the French pilots for its performance. But it cannot be disputed that the type was basically ill-suited for the theatre: its range with payload was too limited for Indo-China (so that only very short loiter times were possible) and its maintenance requirements had been considered in terms of carrier operations (flat decks and manpower-intensive servicing) whereas Indo-China offered poor landing fields and inadequate ground-crew numbers. Thus service-ability was often very low despite the pleas of pilots who loved the Bearcat's low-level manoeuvrability and massive

reserves of power, ideal in mountainous terrain.

But there was nothing that the Bearcat could achieve to prevent the French disaster at Dien Bien Phu in 1954, and as the French pulled out of Indo-China they handed over their surviving Bearcats to the embryonic South Vietnamese air force, which managed to keep the 514th Fighter Squadron operational on the type for some years by cannibalizing remaining aircraft for spare parts.

The only other operator of the Bearcat was the Royal Thai air force after the country had been visited by a US Military Advisory Group in 1950. From 1951 the country received F8F-1D and F8F-1DB aircraft (the totals being 100 and 29 respectively), though only 50 aircraft were delivered in the first year. The F8F-1DBs were eventually cannibalized to keep the F8F-1Ds airworthy, and these aircraft remained in service until the early 1960s with No. 13 Squadron of the 1st Fighter-Bomber Wing and with Nos 22 and 23 Squadrons of the 2nd Fighter-Bomber Wing.

With the Bearcat's gradual phase-out from military service, the type was eagerly accepted as a racing aircraft by wealthy pilots, and Bearcats are still to be seen in drastically modified form in various US air race meetings. But undoubtedly the civilian Bearcat par excellence is the highly modified F8F-2 flown to a world piston-engine speed record by Darryl Greenamyer on 16 August 1969: with each wing clipped by 3 ft 6 in (1.07 m) to reduce span to about 29 ft 0 in (8.84 m), the Pratt & Whitney R-2800-CA18/CB17 uprated to 3,000 hp (2237 kW), the canopy cut down to a small bubble, and empty weight trimmed to some 6,000 lb (2721 kg), this aircraft was named *Conquest 1* and at Edwards Air Force Base streaked over the low-altitude 3-km (1.86-mile) course at 482.462 mph (776.449 km/h) to take the record held since 1939 by Fritz Wendel in a Messerschmitt Me 209. Greenamyer's record stood for some 10 years before being raised to 499.047 mph (803.116 km/h) by a specially modified P-51D Mustang.

# Specifications

## F8F Bearcat variants and production summary

**XF8F-1**: prototypes
| Serial nos | Number | Constr. nos |
|---|---|---|
| 90460/90461 | 2 | D.01/02 |

**F8F-1**: initial production variant
| Serial nos | Number | Constr. nos |
|---|---|---|
| 90437/90459 | 23 | D.1/23 |
| 94752/95498 | 747 | D.24/770 |
| 95499/96751 | 1253 | (cancelled) |
| 100001/102000 | 2000 | (cancelled) |
| 112529/114528 | 2000 | (cancelled) |

**F8F-1B**: cannon-armed derivative of the F8F-1, originally designated **F8F-1C**
| Serial nos | Number | Constr. nos |
|---|---|---|
| 121463/121522 | 60 | D.837/866 |
| 122087/122152 | 66 | D.771/836 |

**F8F-1D**: drone-director conversions of F8F-1s

**F8F-1N**: night-fighter version of F8F-1; two prototype and 36 'production' conversions from F8F-1 fighters

**XF8F-2**: prototype conversions (95049 and 95330) of the F8F-1 for an improved model

**F8F-2**: improved production fighter
| Serial nos | Number | Constr. nos |
|---|---|---|
| 121523/121768 | 246 | D.867/1142 |
| 121769/121780 | 12 | D.1155/1166 |
| 121781/121792 | 12 | D.1175/1186 |
| 122614/122625 | 12 | D.1143/1154 |
| 122626/122633 | 8 | D.1167/1174 |
| 122634/122708 | 75 | D.1187/1261 |

**F8F-2D**: drone-director conversions of F8F-2s

**F8F-2N**: night-fighter version of F8F-2; 12 'production' conversions from F8F-2 fighters

**F8F-2P**: designation of 60 F8F-2s fitted with camera installation and only two wing-mounted cannon

**G-58A**: single civil aircraft for Alford Williams with the name *Gulfhawk 4*

**G-58A Mk II**: single company-owned hybrid F8F-1/F8F-2 aircraft

**F3M-1**: proposed General Motors (Eastern Aircraft Division) production version of the F8F-1; all were cancelled after VJ-Day
| Serial nos | Number |
|---|---|
| 109273/111148 | 1876 |

## F8F-1 Bearcat

**Type:** interceptor fighter and fighter-bomber

**Accommodation:** pilot only

**Armament:** four 0.5-in (12.7-mm) Colt-Browning machine-guns in the wings, plus provision for one 1,600-lb (726-kg) bomb, or two 1,000-lb (454-kg) bomb or four 5-in (127-mm) rockets

**Powerplant:** one 2,100-hp (1566-kW) Pratt & Whitney R-2800-34W radial piston engine with combat ratings of 2,750 hp (2051 kW) at sea level and 2,450 hp (1827 kW) at 9,600 ft (2925 m)

**Performance:**
maximum speed 428 mph (689 km/h) at 18,800 ft (5730 m)
cruising speed: —
initial climb rate 5,610 ft (1710 m) per minute
service ceiling 38,700 ft (11795 m)
range 1,105 miles (1778 km)

**Weights:**
empty equipped 7,323 lb (3322 kg)
normal take-off 9,672 lb (4387 kg)
maximum take-off 12,740 lb (5779 kg)

**Dimensions:**
span 35 ft 6 in (10.82 m)
length 27 ft 8 in (8.43 m)
height 13 ft 8 in (4.16 m)
wing area 244.0 sq ft (22.67 m²)

## F8F-2 Bearcat

**Type:** interceptor fighter and fighter-bomber

**Accommodation** pilot only

**Armament:** four M2 20-mm cannon in the wings, plus provision for one 1,600-lb (726-kg) bomb, or two 1,000-lb (454-kg) bombs or four 5-in (127-mm) rockets

**Powerplant:** one Pratt & Whitney R-2800-30W radial piston engine

**Performance:**
maximum speed 447 mph (720 km/h) at 28,000 ft (8535 m)
cruising speed: —
initial climb rate 4,420 ft (1347 m) per minute
service ceiling 40,700 ft (12405 m)
range 865 miles (1392 km)

**Weights:**
empty equipped 7,690 lb (3488 kg)
normal take-off 10,426 lb (4729 kg)
maximum take-off 13,494 lb (6121 kg)

**Dimensions:**
span 35 ft 10 in (10.92 m) . .
length 28 ft 3 in (8.61 m)
height 13 ft 8 in (4.16 m)
wing area 244.0 sq ft (22.67 m²)

## Conquest 1

**Type:** racing and record-breaking aircraft

**Accommodation:** pilot only

**Armament:** none

**Powerplant:** one 3,000-hp (2237-kW) Pratt & Whitney R-2800-CA18/CB17 radial piston engine

**Performance:**
maximum speed 482.462 mph (776.449 km/h)
cruising speed —
initial climb rate —
service ceiling —
range —

**Weights:**
empty equipped about 6,000 lb (2721 kg)
normal take-off —
maximum take-off —

**Dimensions:**
length about 29 ft 0 in (8.84 m)
length about 30 ft 0 in (9.14 m)
height 13 ft 10 in (4.22 m)
wing area —

## F8F-1B Bearcat

**Type:** interceptor fighter and fighter-bomber

**Accommodation:** pilot only

**Armament:** four M2 20-mm cannon in the wings, plus provision for one 1,600-lb (726-kg) bomb, or two 1,000-lb (454-kg) bombs or four 5-in (127-mm) rockets

**Powerplant:** same as F8F-1

**Performance:**
maximum speed 425 mph (684 km/h) at 18,800 ft (5730 m)
cruising speed —
initial climb rate 5,310 ft (1618 m) per minute
service ceiling 38,000 ft (17235 m)
range —

**Weights:**
empty equipped 7,765 lb (3522 kg)
normal take-off 9,672 lb (4387 kg)
maximum take-off 12,740 lb (5779 kg)

**Dimensions:**
span 35 ft 6 in (10.82 m)
length 27 ft 8 in (8.43 m)
height 13 ft 8 in (4.16 m)
wing area 244.0 sq ft (22.67 m²)

## XF8F-1 Bearcat

**Type:** prototype interceptor fighter

**Accommodation:** pilot only

**Armament:** four 0.5-in (12.7-mm) Colt-Browning machine-guns in the wings

**Powerplant:** one 2,100-hp (1566-kW) Pratt & Whitney R-2800-22W radial piston engine

**Performance:**
maximum speed 424 mph (682 km/h) at 17,300 ft (5275 m)
cruising speed —
initial climb rate 4,800 ft (1463 m) per minute
service ceiling —
range 600 miles (966 km)

**Weights:**
empty equipped 6,733 lb (3054 kg)
normal take-off 8,788 lb (3986 kg)
maximum take-off —

**Dimensions:**
span 35 ft 6 in (10.82 m)
length 27 ft 8 in (8.43 m)
height 13 ft 8 in (4.16 m)
wing area 244.0 sq ft (22.67 m²)

## ACKNOWLEDGEMENTS

The author wishes to thank the following for supplying illustrations:
Candid Aero-Files: p. 24 (both).
James Gilbert: pp. 4/5, 8, 9, 10, 12, 14, 15, 16, 25, 30, 35 (bottom), 36, 37, 40 (both), 41, 43, 52/53, 54 (bottom).
Mike Jerram: pp. 13, 19 (inset), 20, 21 (top), 22 (both), 23 (both), 26 (both), 27 (both), 28, 29 (both), 35 (top), 38/39, 42, 44/45, 46, 47, 51 (bottom), 54 (top).
Military Archive and Research Services: 11, 18/19, 21 (bottom), 32, 48/49, 48 (inset), 50, 51 (top).
L. P. Nolan: p. 17 (both).

In their aerial element, F8F-1 Bearcats
from a US Navy escort carrier formate
closely for the camera..